COMMUNICATION

In

MARRIAGE

How to Communicate With Your Spouse
Without Fighting

By: Marcus and Ashley Kusi

Publishing services provided by  **Archangel Ink**

ISBN: 0692452141
ISBN-13: 9780692452141

Disclaimer

The views expressed are those of the authors alone, and should not be taken as expert advice. The information here is intended for informative purposes. The reader is responsible for his or her own actions.

We share what we have learned in life and marriage, therefore if any of the information in this book comes out as advice, please take it as a grain of salt.

About the Authors

Marcus and Ashley help newlyweds adjust to married life, and provide married couples with resources for building a strong foundation for their marriage.

We do this by using our own marriage experience, that of great married couples, and sharing what works for us through our website and marriage podcast, The First Year Marriage Show.

Visit the website below to listen to the podcast.

www.firstyearmarriage.com

Visit our website to learn more about us.

www.ourpeacefulfamily.com

Your FREE Gift

As a special THANK YOU for buying this book, we created a 7-Day Worksheet to help you implement the 7 simple steps included in this book.

All you have to do is join our subscriber's list by submitting your email address.

Visit www.ourpeacefulfamily.com/7dayworksheet to get your copy.

Table of Contents

Introduction

Where do you think you fall on the zero to ten scale of communication?

Everything that we do in life involves some form of communication. We have even tried to think of some aspect of marriage that didn't involve communication and we came up with nothing. Money, everyday life, career, food, sex…it all involves communication. Why? Because no one can read your mind!

Whether you are having trouble communicating, or just want to improve your communication by moving from good to great, this book will provide helpful information and actionable steps to help you implement these strategies in your relationship.

Communicating with your spouse is not talking about the good stuff only, or when things are good. It also involves talking about the bad things and when everything seems to be falling apart. Coming together to develop a plan of action will help you to communicate through both. How can you fix your marriage problems if you do not communicate with each other? You will have unresolved conflicts, be unfulfilled in your marriage, and always be thinking "is this what marriage is supposed to be?"

These marriage problems will build up over time and explode someday. When this happens, it will not be pretty. You certainly want to avoid it! You want to be able to communicate with your spouse so you can both have a fulfilling marriage, the marriage you both dreamed about before saying, 'I Do.'

Poor communication can lead to growing apart as a couple. It also impacts your kids since they will be learning from you. So, teach them how to do it in a healthy way by communicating well with your spouse. This is a simple thing but requires your action and effort to make it happen.

When you are able to communicate effectively with your spouse, you will feel secure. You will not be afraid to ask questions or seek answers. And you will have a higher level of fulfillment in your marriage.

Effective communication is one of the major life lessons we all need to learn. It's vital for a great marriage, and goes hand in hand with a healthy one. It's the key to a successful marriage. Effective communication means you both understand each other when you communicate. The earlier you learn how to communicate with your spouse, the better off your marriage will be. Why? Because communication problems are the main reasons, or root cause, of the top issues that could cause married couples to divorce, separate, or breed unhealthy relationships.

There are many degrees of communication, from bad, to better, to effective. We want to walk you through the simple strategies we have implemented in our marriage and had success with in terms of how we communicate with each other as a married couple.

We learned these strategies from personal practice, by watching and listening to other couples, and reading. Whether or not you choose to become a better communicator is fully up to you. It takes work and may be uncomfortable at times, but it will all be worth it for your marriage.

Have you ever witnessed a married couple who have had obvious communication issues? It isn't pretty. What you may not realize is that a lot of seemingly unrelated issues stem from the lack of effective communication. Money issues, fights over being too busy, not busy enough, who does what around the house, starting a family, how many children to have, sex, connecting together, parenting, intimacy…Starting to get the picture?

Communication is integral to everything you do with your spouse and in your marriage.

In order to improve communication in your marriage the desire and willingness of you and your spouse is needed. It will take intentional effort from you and your spouse to communicate better in your marriage.

By learning how to communicate effectively with your spouse, you will be able to succeed in your marriage, do things you never thought possible, and excel in all different areas of your life. Marriage is one of the greatest growing opportunities we have on this earth. It has its ups and downs, but the important thing is to learn how to grow closer together through it all as a unit. First, you need to understand some key things that play a huge role when it comes to communication in marriage.

For example: Know why you communicate and what you are communicating about. There will be days when you will simply sit and talk about a TV show, sports, family events, work etc., talks that do not require setting a time and place! There will also be days when you have the "we need to talk" conversation. With conversations like these, you both need to know why you need to talk so you can prepare well ahead of time. It might not be what you both wanted, but it could be the beginning of something great for your marriage. In situations like this, knowing your 'why' for the conversation will set you up to focus on the issue at hand, which will enable you to come to a compromise or resolution without having to waste time talking about irrelevant things.

We have to talk about the small stuff before it becomes the big stuff that ruins our marriage.

CHAPTER 1

Men and Women Communicate Differently

We learned it first hand in the beginning of our marriage, and it was quite shocking how truly different we communicate. In our marriage, Marcus is more logical and less emotional when it comes to decisions, while Ashley can be both logical and emotional, but tends to be more emotional.

For example:

If we get invited somewhere for a gathering, and Marcus has work he needs to finish, other plans, or is just not in the mood, he will quickly say, "No thank you." He is also more of an introvert. On the other hand, I may think of the countless times we already turned previous invitations down, and feel like we should say 'yes,' or just want to get out of the house! - Ashley

Neither is the right way or the wrong way; each is simply different because we have different personalities. There is a time and place for both ways; we just had to find the balance.

When it comes to how we spend our money, create a budget, make plans and goals, typically logical thinking takes the lead. When it comes to advising each other, listening to each other's struggles, point of view, hopes and dreams, it's usually more emotional than just logic.

Communication can be vastly different for men and women. You have to remember your spouse may share a lot of qualities that you can generalize with their sex, but in the end you need to think of them as the exception; so learn your spouse's communication style in speech behavior and their love language. (If you do not know the love language of your spouse, get a copy of this book, 'The Five Love Languages,' by Dr. Gary Chapman).

Quality time is part of Ashley's love language, so I make it a priority to give her that every day. Sometimes she will say, "Come snuggle me," thinking I am going to come right away to snuggle her. Although I will answer and say yes, I might take a minute or two…or twenty before I go snuggle her. Her expectation was for me to come right away.

Sometimes we use the same words, but they have different meaning to each of us. She meant at that moment, I meant in a few minutes once I was finished with what I was doing. - Marcus

Learning that men and women think and communicate differently is key to effective and efficient communication in marriage. *We also express our emotions very differently.* Therefore, you have to be aware that your tone and choice of the words you use affects the actual content you are trying to communicate to your spouse. Sometimes the tone of your voice is more important than the actual words you say.

Non-Verbal Communication: Body Language

Let's start by explaining exactly what non-verbal communication is:

"To make the meaning of our words clear we use body language. Body language is a language without spoken words and is therefore called non-verbal communication. We use body language all the time. For instance, looking someone in the eyes means something different than not looking someone in the eyes. In contact with others, it 's just not possible to not be communicating something. Usually body language occurs unconsciously. Yet the body language we use decides to a large extent the quality of our communication. "(Frank van Marwijk)

Body language plays a huge role in communication in general, which makes it that much more important when you communicate with your spouse, the one who knows you best. Specifically, somewhere around ninety percent of our daily communication is through body language. You probably didn't realize non-verbal communication played such a gigantic role when you have conversations, did you? The numbers are staggering. We tell you this so you can get an idea of how important it is for you to be aware of how you are non-verbally and verbally communicating with your spouse, as well as how your spouse is communicating to you.

For example:

Marcus will ask me if I'm okay, and I will say, "Fine," although my body is stiff, and I won't look at him. In the beginning of our marriage he would just believe my "fine" and go about his business. I had to learn to communicate verbally and it was so hard for me at first. The root of that was I felt vulnerable and although my husband is the one person I should feel the safest being vulnerable with, my past and insecurities kept me guarded still.
– Ashley

Most Common Communication Problem That Happens In Marriage

The following experience seems to be quite common. A wife comes up to her husband and just wants to vent and express her problem, only wanting her husband to sympathize with her. Instead of just the, "Gee honey, I'm really sorry to hear that," that she wants to hear; her husband sees a problem and looks for a solution. He responds, "Well, if you stop doing X," or "Just don't be friends with her anymore." Men are typically problem solvers by nature and women are more nurturing, or natural sympathizers. It does not imply that women cannot solve problems and men cannot sympathize. We have to learn each other's strong suits and tendencies.

I have learned to verbalize my feelings, and what I am trying to communicate to my husband more. I have learned to be more logical in my thinking in the areas of my life that need it. I have learned my husband can't read my mind. - Ashley

I have learned to ask my wife if she just needs to have me sympathize with her or help come up with a solution. If it is something we need solutions for, we quickly devise a plan to help her or discuss the issue. - Marcus

So what happens when you absolutely cannot communicate a thought to your spouse? This can be very frustrating and we have learned a few things in this department. First, you have to be assertive. By assertive, we don't mean forceful. Rather, less emotional and more logical in the sense that your goal is now to help each other understand exactly what you mean, and exactly what your spouse means.

You can use strategies talked about in the Empathetic Listening chapter, as well as trying to draw diagrams, writing on paper etc., to communicate well to your spouse. Depending on what you are trying to communicate, try different verbal explanations. Get creative.

Never just assume you know what your spouse is trying to convey to you, especially when you feel hurt. Don't take things personal until you clarify that's what your spouse intended.

You can ask clarifying questions like:

❖ This is what I feel like you are saying. Is this what you mean?

❖ What do you mean by this word?

❖ How does this make you feel when I say…?

❖ What do you think I mean when I say…?

We have used these communication strategies several times to improve communication in our marriage. These are strategies we actively put to use in our marriage every day and we stand by them.

Love and Respect

"Wives need love and husbands need respect." Dr. Emerson Eggerichs

Your marriage needs both love and respect towards each other when you communicate, especially for you to make it through those tough and sensitive conversations like sex, late payments, debt, money, in-laws, religion, kids, and everything else we deal with in life.

Typically the wife will desire more love, as the husband will crave more respect during these sensitive conversations. Each is equally important in your marriage relationship. Now let's talk about how this affects your communication with each other.

Dictionary.com defines respect as, "Esteem for or a sense of the worth or excellence of a person…the condition of being esteemed or honored…a formal expression or gesture of greeting, esteem, or friendship…favor or partiality."

Your spouse should be your best friend, the person you hold a special place in your heart for, the person you decided to devote your life to.

We should give them the respect they need and vice versa. Mutual respect helps you not to take advantage of your spouse. When you respect your spouse in the way you speak to them, the way you speak about them to other people, and the way you treat them, it will help your marriage move from good to great. Both spouse's need respect, but this is especially true for husbands. Communicating with respect towards your spouse will help them do the same for you.

Respect is usually earned, but sometimes it requires us to give it without being deserved. If you respond to your spouse with respect even when they may not be worthy of it, you will have accomplished an act of selflessness. If both you and your spouse work on being respectful, not only to each other as you communicate, but also when you talk about your spouse to other people, you're cultivating an honoring relationship.

The term, "Telling the truth in kindness," comes to mind. You have to be honest and respectful at the same time as you communicate with your spouse.

You need to treat him/her with the esteem you also want to be given. Respect in the way you take care of yourself. Respect in the way you spend money. Honoring your spouse in the way you behave with other people, or when you are alone. Affection in the way you respond to your husband or wife. Show respect with what you watch or read.

Pornography and reading sexually explicit books is an example of being disrespectful. (You might not agree with this, and that's okay). If your spouse is not okay with it, you need to be respectful of that. It is really about talking and figuring out how exactly each of you feels both respected and disrespected.

When you do or say things, keep in mind the question, *how would my spouse feel if I did this? Would they feel respected? How would I feel if they did this?*

Love. It seems to be what a lot of our life revolves around. The human connection associated with love is what helps us as humans feel we have a purpose. Sometimes love can hurt, but we want to help you learn how to communicate in love so that there will be less injury. Communicating in love starts with remembering to think about what you say or do before you do it, wanting the best for your spouse, and keeping that at the forefront of your mind at all times. You are not without fault and neither is your spouse, so give them the same grace you would want. It will not be easy if you are not used to thinking about your spouse a lot, but you can do it.

You can show them love in both sexual and nonsexual touches, helping around the house, gifts, quality time with no distractions, in the way you speak, compliments, and so much more. For further ideas on showing love, you have to find out what both you and your spouse's love language are. We recommend you to read, 'The Five Love Languages' by Gary Chapman.

Making your spouse feel loved can be an awesome gift to your spouse. You can sit down with them and ask them when and how they most feel loved. Ask them to think of a time they felt loved by you and pay attention to the details. Is it something you said? Something you did? Another way you can show love is trying to express your love for your spouse in different ways and see which they like more.

Ask yourself and your spouse:

1. How do you feel most loved by your spouse?
2. How do you feel most respected by your spouse?
3. How do you feel unloved?
4. How do you feel disrespected?

Thinking of a specific incidence between the two of you may help.

CHAPTER 2

Learn How To Listen To Your Spouse

The first part of communication may be a surprise for you to hear (no pun intended). It's the art of listening and paying attention. Yes, the first step to properly communicate with your spouse is to learn how to practice *empathetic listening*.

Have you caught yourself trying to think of your response and reply while listening to your spouse? You are not really listening to them because you are more concerned about them understanding you.

Over the years, we have learned to solely devote our attention to listening until the end of a statement before thinking about responding. We try to see things through each other's eyes. Not that we have perfected it, but we have both grown to be a lot better at it. Empathy is defined as, "Identification with an understanding of another's situation, feelings, and motives." (Free Dictionary) This means you should be trying to understand and see where your spouse is coming from, where they are at, and why they feel the way they do.

Empathic listening is simply listening with empathy. It does not mean you have to automatically agree with your spouse. It means trying to understand them and putting yourself in their shoes. By listening empathically to each other, our communication has improved in a big way.

"The biggest problem in communication is we do not listen to understand…we listen to reply." Unknown

This quote explains empathetic listening in a nutshell. It's really the foundation of communication. When you try to open yourself up to the possibility that there may be another way of looking at things, you will understand that your spouse has equal rights, opposing thoughts, and feelings which helps you to grow. Listening empathetically helps you to understand your spouse on a deeper level. This also helps you from being egocentric, moving from *I* to *WE*.

One classic example to illustrate empathic listening is this:

Men usually listen and try to give a solution. Husbands try to fix every problem their wives come to them with, whereas their wives only want them to listen to their situation and say, "I'm sorry you have to deal with that."

There is a time and place to give solutions or listen empathically. What works best is to make your intentions clear, "Honey, I just need you to listen to me. Just let me vent." Or, "I need your help to find a solution to this." When you have a disagreement, remember, empathetic listening can go a long way. Learn how to listen to your spouse by paying attention to them, giving them the full attention they deserve and learning to be quiet. Silence on your part will help you to listen well.

When you both have the opportunity to explain why you feel so strongly about your opinion, and want your spouse to clearly understand your point of view, make sure only one of you speaks whiles the other listens. Sometimes it means raising your hand and saying who should talk and who should listen. You should make an effort to understand your spouse.

You don't want your spouse preparing to respond instead of completely listening to you. The next time you have a conversation or talk with your spouse, try to empathetically listen to them, and see what results you get. We think you might be surprised.

Remember, give your spouse grace, as you yourself need it, to grow and improve as a person and as a spouse. One way to help each other along the way is to give each other words of encouragement. *If you are busy trying to uplift your spouse and support them, having patience with them becomes second nature.*

Actively Listening

"There is a voice that doesn't use words. Listen." Rumi

How do you feel when you try to tell your spouse something while they are watching TV or on their phone? You don't get a response, or you get a, "Wait, what?" Then you have to repeat yourself, and feel like you are not being heard, listened to, or like your spouse doesn't get you. This happened often for us. And after a while, we learned that we were doing this to each other, and it was causing communication issues to say the least. If your spouse is not looking at you, they are most likely not listening to you. Make sure you look at each other while you are talking so you can listen and give your full attention to your spouse. We like to call this face-time.

Get to the point if you can as quickly as possible, and keep it simple. There are some things you can explain in a few sentences, whiles other things will require some minutes, hours, or an overnight. For the things that you can explain in a sentence or two, do not waste time trying to say it in 30 minutes. Example, "Did you wash the dishes?" For the things that require longer the a few sentences, try to schedule time to talk about them. For example, "How did we go wrong with the budget?"

Staying on topic. It's very easy to start bringing past unresolved issues into the mix during conversations, which can lead to not only forgetting what you are discussing, but also decreasing the time you've already allocated to each other. If what you are discussing is a result of some past unresolved issues, try to figure out whether you will both be better off discussing and resolving your past issues before tackling newer issues.

A Few Things We Did That You Can Also Do

❖ Pay more attention to your spouse before you start the conversation. Are they in the middle of something?

❖ Lay your hand on their arm or leg to get their attention.

❖ Say, "Honey, let me know when you're ready to listen because I have something I need to tell you/talk about."

❖ Try to be more attentive to your spouse's voice and the tone they use.

❖ Don't put up any walls to prevent yourself from listening and understanding what your spouse is talking to you about.

❖ Have an open mind.

❖ Learn how to listen with your ears and watch for body language with your eyes. (When you talk to your supervisor, or have a job interview, you look in their eyes, so why not look in your spouse's eyes?)

❖ Be interested in what your spouse has to say.

These few things have helped us in a big way. We are definitely not perfect in this department, but we are both trying and that's what matters.

It is so very important to actively listen to each other because it makes the other person feel validated, respected, loved, and heard.

CHAPTER 3

Patience

Patience is another critical factor for a healthy, happy, and successful marriage. Patience helps us to communicate without getting angry easily. It is the ability to tolerate and restrains you from reacting in anger or frustration.

Have you ever had a slow computer, or a computer that takes its sweet time to load after turning it on? What did you do when the computer was being slow? You either waited patiently or began to complain about this computer being slow, maybe clicked vigorously, or slammed something. In either situation, did the computer perform any faster for you? The obvious answer is no, but either waiting with patience or complaining had two different effects on you.

By being patient for the computer to load, your mood was calm and positive. But when you complained and clicked several times your mood was more aggressive. Based on this example alone, we can all realize that being patient will provide us with a more positive mood and outcome.

So what does patience in marriage mean? How can it help you communicate better with your spouse? It means being patient with your spouse and your marriage. It means you have to be patient with your spouse when they hurt or make you angry unintentionally, and when your marriage is not what you want it to be.

Imagine yourself belittling or yelling at your spouse just because you were angry about something trivial they did. Now imagine you are in their position, and you are the one getting yelled at or belittled. Not a great feeling right? The golden rule applies here, so decide to try and treat your spouse the same way you want to be treated. Respect and love your spouse!

There are many instances that patience can be implemented when communicating with your spouse. It is an everyday need. Here are a few examples:

- ❖ When you are having a disagreement with your spouse.
- ❖ When your spouse doesn't seem to be paying attention to you.
- ❖ When your spouse wants to wait until the game is over to take the trash out.
- ❖ When your spouse takes a long time to get ready to leave, making you late.

See how you could easily become angry based on the above examples? Being patient with your spouse allows you to think about your choice of words when responding to them. Taking that extra pause helps you be more aware of your tone and if you are getting angry. That additional moment you take to be patient helps you so you do not respond in a defensive reaction. You can find many instances everyday where you can practice being patient, especially with your spouse.

A good example is that you need to have patience when it comes to disagreeing with your spouse. Sometimes you have to pause and come back to the conversation after you cool down, have time to think, and for your spouse to do the same. Having patience in that instance can be challenging if you like to resolve things quickly and not leave things for an amount of time. Just to let you know, not everything can be resolved before you go to bed, sometimes you might have to wait until the next morning to resolve it, or seek help from someone.

You also have to have patience when timing conversations that you know may be more involved. It is best to wait to have a deeper conversation, or one that may involve some emotional strain for when you are both relaxed and have a moment to yourselves.

For example, we like to prepare each other by saying, "Honey, I want to talk to you about something, so let me know when you are ready." You can give them a hint as to what topic it is about like sex, rent, work schedule, etc.

Patience towards your spouse allows you to think, most importantly, before you react. Having patience with each other will help you to communicate without fighting, argue less, and have calm discussions. It certainly encourages good communication in marriage.

In our first year of marriage, I will admit I did not have much (if any) patience. Marcus had a lot of it. Eventually his patience did rub off on me. I have since learned and grown in my patience. I came to realize if he snapped at me as much or as quickly as I did to him, I would feel incredibly hurt. So why would I continue to do this to him? A big apology was in order, and I began the hard journey of learning patience in marriage.
- Ashley

Remember to take a pause when you feel the emotions rising so you don't just react. Patience takes time and practice to learn. It will not happen overnight!

"Patience is bitter, but its fruit is sweet." Jean-Jacques Rousseau

Ask yourself and your spouse:

1. What can you do to have more patience with your spouse?

2. What are five things you love about your spouse? Think on the positive when you feel negative.

3. Can you think of a time you lost your patience with your spouse? What was the trigger? What was the root of what set you off?

4. How can you do better next time?

CHAPTER 4

Your Expectations Affects How You Communicate

Marriage expectations are one of the things you don't really learn about until you have been married for a little while. It's another one of those things you may be told about, but not really understand until you are in the thick of things with your spouse. You have to talk about your marriage expectations, especially how you communicate, because it is much easier to understand where your spouse is coming from and what they are trying to communicate to you, when you know their expectations.

We all grew up in homes that will always be different from our spouse's. For us, it was entirely different cultures as well. If your parents and people very close to you did not communicate well, you are likely to communicate just like them. Communicate openly about everything and anything. Try to remember that communication is a learned skill, and probably won't happen overnight.

In my family the men are the ones who take care of the car, such as oil changes, car repairs, tire changes, etc. They usually repair stuff and do the stereotypical "masculine" jobs.

An exception to this is my mother who does absolutely everything she can because she had to as a single parent. In the beginning of our marriage something in my brain clicked: "Yay! I don't have to worry about changing the oil or tires anymore!"

I quickly got aggravated that my husband didn't know the first thing about cars. He came from a family that did not own a car, in fact a lot of people in his country don't because they are too expensive and a hassle.

I had to teach him how to drive, change a tire, check the oil, and maintain the car. He now understands what my expectation was, and he looks forward to taking care of it. I didn't even realize I had this and many other unconscious marriage expectations; specifically these role expectations.
– Ashley

Your environment, past experiences, relationships, parents, grandparents, whether present or absent, played a certain role in your life. And shaped your marriage expectations in the way you think about the roles a husband and wife should play. How they communicate with each other, who should lead, and who should follow during certain times. These past experiences have also shaped you to communicate in a certain way be it verbally or non-verbally, and once you are married; you will have to learn how to communicate with your spouse. That is why it is very crucial to explore and discuss the way you each think about communication.

When communicating with in-laws, it's best if you each speak to your side of the family when dealing with potentially conflicting subjects, while maintaining a united front.

An example of this would be when we named our daughter. Some of Marcus's relatives desired a different middle name than we did. We decided what we wanted to name her, and then Marcus talked to his relatives about it, telling them what we chose.

With my family it was more about social events and boundary setting. We chose what events we would fit into our schedule and not do things at the drop of a hat. I was the one that spoke to them and let them know if we could or couldn't make it. – Ashley

Since your past communication experience has a direct impact on how you communicate, sit down with your spouse to talk about how your parents, relatives, friends, and role models communicated with each other and with you. Now discuss how you think and feel about communication based on your past. Does it have to involve shouting, yelling, fighting, criticism, and throwing things against the wall? Does it have to be calm and respectful? You get the idea.

By doing this you will both have a better idea on your thoughts about communication, and will be able to identify the best way the two of you can communicate with each other without having to worry about whose method of communication is right or wrong. Knowing your communication styles will make things easier for your marriage.

For example:

When we got married I expected my wife to do most of the cooking, washing the dishes, making the bed each morning, laundry, etc. I knew how to do all of these things, but in my culture it is usually the women that handle all of these. - Marcus

This may sound like we are a couple from the 1950s, so let us share some other expectations we had for each other with you and how they affected the way we communicated with each other.

I had a deal breaker that any man I would marry HAD to view men and women equally! Just because I wanted to be a stay-at-home mother and he wanted to be the main bread winner didn't mean we saw either of us having a bigger say in things. Equality in opinions and worth was an expectation of mine that I shared before we got married; luckily my husband shared the same view. I expected to be treated as an equal because that was actually the opposite in a lot of my upbringing. By communicating this to him, we were able to resolve some of the issues easily as we both had this equal responsibilities mindset. – Ashley

I expected Ashley to view life the same way I did. I thought we would be in agreement with how we dealt with our money, never borrowing or using credit. That was not the case. I expected her to see things through my eyes.

I had to learn that I needed to accept that we will always be different, and that's a good thing. By accepting that we will always be different, we have been able to communicate better on various issues that we have encountered in our marriage. – Marcus

We had to communicate our expectations and discover we both had very different ideas when it came to how we communicate, spend money, sex, duties, roles, how often we would be social and go out to do things, meet emotional needs, faith, resolving conflicts, and so much more. You need to identify what communication expectations you have for your spouse, then have a conversation with them. Communicate to each other, not only what communication expectations you have, but why you have them. What do they mean to you?

For example, your spouse has the day off and in your mind, you are figuring they will have the house cleaned and some other things done that need to be accomplished. You go to work and come back to absolutely nothing done that you expected to be taken care of. You're mad now, but do you have a right to be?

Did you communicate to your spouse about your expectation that they would have completed this mental To Do list of yours?

Your spouse is not in your mind and as a result, you must not assume they know what's in your head. Your spouse is not a mind reader! That is why discussing your expectations to your spouse is an important part of communication in marriage. Having unrealistic expectations will also increase the chances of your ideals being unmet. Remember, you cannot change your spouse, only yourself. You need to come to a compromise about your communication expectations, and expectations for your marriage, as you have equal say in it.

At the end of the year, we usually talk about what goals we have for the following year, what big-ticket items we want to buy, and how much we expect to spend on them. Usually our ideas are very different in terms of how much to spend, but by communicating through them, we find a compromise. Communicating about your expectations and desires is essential throughout your marriage.

With patience, compromise, understanding, listening and teamwork, you will be on your way to resolving your communication expectations.

Sexpectations

Yes, your expectations about sex. Did you know that you and your spouse will probably have different expectations about sex in your marriage? Did you know your expectation of how often you want to have sex would also change in the different seasons of your life?

Communicate to your spouse how often you would like to make love, see how often they want to, and compromise on a frequency.

Just as you have expectations of how often you will make love, you have expectations of the kind of sex you want to have. Again, this will change throughout your life, and you need to remember to communicate to your spouse as your expectations evolve. This is not just a one-time conversation; you will continually need to communicate about your expectations and desires all throughout your marriage. Knowing each other's communication style (the way you each communicate) will be make it easier to communicate effectively without fighting.

Quick Tip: Have a joint calendar or something to know what you are each doing, places or events to go, food to eat, etc. This makes it easy to communicate during the day and also plan ahead of time.

If you are going to be late at work, don't wait until the last hour before you let your spouse know. Tell them in advance. The best time is the moment you find out you will be late coming home. It will help your spouse to prepare well ahead for you. It will help you stay united and be well informed.

Ask yourself and your spouse:

1. How do your parents, or parental role models in your life communicate?

2. What do you like/dislike about how they communicate?

3. How do you communicate like them?

4. How do you communicate differently from them?

5. What is one thing you can do to adopt a better communication style, and cleave from the negative path you usually take?

CHAPTER 5

How to Communicate Through Conflict

Attack the problem, not the person.

Disagreeing with your spouse from time to time is inevitable. You are two different people with two unique personalities, thoughts, and opinions. You both have equal rights and responsibilities in your marriage relationship. Your opinions matter equally.

The tough part is learning how to disagree in a respectful and healthy way, or as we like to call it: fighting fair.

When you learn how to communicate through your disagreement and differences in a positive way, you can both come through it stronger. By doing this, you will grow together and continue to learn about your spouse. If done in a respectful way, fighting fair in your marriage can be one of the best things for your marriage. And there will be plenty of opportunities for you to disagree with your spouse right from the beginning.

How you do the dishes, load the dishwasher, fold laundry, hang the toilet paper, squeeze the toothpaste, split up household responsibilities and spend your money will be some of the common things you can butt heads on. Just remember we are all human and therefore, we are imperfect.

When I think of fighting fair in marriage, I'm brought back to how my parents fought growing up, as well as the many other couples I was exposed to. There was plenty of screaming, name-calling, yelling, things being thrown, and physical abuse. As a result of this experience, I thought this was how couples fought with each other whenever they had disagreement. After we got married, I thought that when we disagreed on something, the name calling and belittling would be normal. I didn't realize this was a marriage expectation I had.

Marcus never, not once, let his temper (he has one it just rarely comes out) get the best of him to the point of him calling me a name or belittling me. He would sometimes say, "I need you to stop talking to me and leave me alone before I say something we will both regret."

That statement alone taught me so much! Wait, we don't have to do anything like name calling? We don't have to yell? We won't hurt each other and have to apologize for things we didn't mean later? It was a paradigm shift for me and immensely increased my respect for Marcus.

I was the hot-tempered, fly-off-the-handle type in the first few months of our marriage. But I've now learned how to take a deep breath, and not just react, but to think it through first.

Just like any married couple, we have disagreements from time to time.

Sometimes we have to just agree to disagree on certain topics, or give each other time and space, and revisit later once we both have had time to let our emotions die down and we've had time to think. - Ashley

Yelling and name-calling are not going to help you be heard any better than allow you to understand where your spouse is coming from. You don't have to continue the cycle and include shouting and belittling into the disagreements you have with your spouse.

Resolving Your Differences

Having different perspectives is okay. You can be a Party A supporter and your spouse could be Party B supporter. That's fine because you will never agree on everything. Use your differences to have a healthy discussion and see how your strengths compliment's each other's weaknesses.

Sometimes you will have an overload of stress from work, family errands, relatives, in-laws, the kids, and your spouse will get the brunt of it. You have to remember to take a pause when you feel like you are being impatient, angry, and reacting too quickly with them. This is a lifelong practice. Ultimately you want the best for each other, which in turn, works out to be the best for the both of you as a unit. You just have to learn to let go sometimes and cut your spouse some slack. You are not your spouse's parent!

You need to diffuse the situation when you realize you are not effectively communicating any longer with your spouse and take a step back. Take a break from the conversation if you are getting upset or tired. Be aware of your tone and attitude when disagreeing. Are you being open-minded and trying to see things through your spouse's eyes?

Remember, give your spouse the same amount of respect you desire and treat them the way you want to be treated. **If you cannot compromise or agree, take a break.** Sometimes you may have to revisit a conflict a few times, or give it a day or so; it really depends on the issue. The key is to be respectful, loving, open-minded, and true to yourself while respecting your spouse's different perspectives.

When resolving conflicts, try to talk in a calming voice; no shouting and yelling. Never raise your voice. When you raise your voice, your tone changes which can put your spouse on the defense. Your spouse will not be open to receiving what you are saying. Understand that you do not have to resolve a conflict on a first try. Sometimes you will need a few days or months to make a decision. Just make sure you both have a timeline or date by which you will have to make a decision together.

Don't compare your spouse to another person when you are communicating, especially in a heated argument. An example, "You are just like your father!" "You just don't want to do this because your mother doesn't want you to." Respect your spouse's feelings and opinions. Don't avoid those difficult discussions like whether to circumcise your child, where to live, which house to buy, or any of the discussions that you would label as challenging. If you are nagging and complaining every time, put an end to it. No one wants to be with someone who does that all the time. Do you? It helps if you both agree on a time frame that you can both take a break from the topic for a while to get some perspective, gain some knowledge, and come to a compromise. Pick a deadline and create some boundaries. Choose a period of time you will break from the subject until a certain date.

At the first sign that we are disagreeing on something and I feel that frustration starting, I stop and take a deep breath. I clear my head and decide to have an open mind. Then I will usually ask Marcus to explain clearly what he means or why he is thinking this way so I can understand where he is coming from. Most of our disagreements are results of misunderstandings and this is one way to clear it up. - Ashley

Whenever we have a conflict, I ensure I am calm, relaxed, and patient. I try my best to listen and to understand Ashley's point of view. Sometimes I will not get it the first time, but after further explanation I am able to understand what she means. If it's a heated argument, I take some time to calm down and think about the issue before we even work on a compromise.

It's not easy having conflicts with Ashley, but we have learned that, having conflicts is part of married life. - Marcus

If you feel you have the same argument frequently or just a lot of disagreements, sit down and find the root cause of these conflicts. Could it be poor communication, a misunderstanding, miscommunication, or poor decision-making? Don't let something that is bothering you fester. Spend time with your spouse talking about the issues affecting your marriage. Don't keep it all in by avoiding to deal with your issues head on. Always be looking for ways to improve your marriage. Ask your spouse, "What did you mean by this? I know you didn't mean to hurt me, but I felt X when you said this, or did this."

** Major conflicts that have to do with moral issues, or conflicts that involve safety of you, your spouse, someone else involved, or children are a little different. There is a right and a wrong. This isn't a one size fits all and you should seek the help of the proper authorities.

If you both try to see things from each other's perspectives and have an open mind, take a turn speaking, practice empathetic and active listening, have a healthy debate until the conflict is resolved or you can find a compromise, you will be well on your way to communicating effectively in your marriage. If you have unresolved issues, today is the day to talk about them and resolve them one at a time. When conflicts in your marriage are resolved in a mature, respectful and mutual manner, it will serve as an opportunity to grow.

7 Steps for Resolving Your Differences

1. Have an open mind. Drop any pre-conceived notions you have that will prevent you from talking, discussing, and resolving conflicts with your spouse.
2. Commit to solving the conflict or problem you have.
3. Pay attention and listen when your spouse is talking. Don't just assume you know what they mean and how they feel.
4. Identify the root cause of the conflict and have a clear understanding of the conflict before trying to resolve it. Attack the problem, not the person.
5. Take responsibility for your actions and emotions. Don't be defensive about them; be accountable.
6. Be willing to forgive your spouse, or ask for forgiveness.
7. Find solutions, compromise (a common ground), and implement the solutions you both agreed upon.

Keeping Score

Keeping score is very crippling for a healthy marriage. Do not keep score with who was wrong! *Marriage is not a competition between husband and wife.* Marriage is a team sport where two unique individuals come together to win together in life. You should have each other's good in mind and be thinking of how you can make your spouse feel more loved. If one of you is winning, so is the other. In the same way, if one of you is losing, the other is as well.

One example would be when you have the argument in your head before you bring it up to your spouse. You have played the scene in your mind, so you know what you are going to say, how your spouse is most likely to respond, and how you can prove your point to "win". If you're always trying to one up on your spouse, it makes your relationship ripe for conflict. This is the man or woman you want to spend the rest of your life with, so find a compromise. Do not compete!

We are imperfect humans who are born egocentric. Learning to not be selfish takes time and practice. You have to forgive and let go because you want your spouse to do the same for you, right? Did you know keeping score with your spouse's wrong doings and holding them over their head is a form of manipulation? It sure isn't helping you communicate effectively either. Your spouse does not owe you anything for making a mistake or being wrong. In the same way, you don't owe them. So don't try to guilt your spouse into doing things that they, as a free and independent person, doesn't want to do. Each situation is different and should be treated as such. In some instances you will have to come out of your comfort zone and so will your spouse.

I realized I would try to get Marcus to go somewhere with me by saying "You never do X, I really want you to go with me and spend time with your wife." I honestly didn't realize that I was trying to play with his emotions to guilt him into going with me.

After I realized I was not respecting his boundaries and actually manipulating him, I paid a lot more attention to the words I used when I wanted him to do something or go somewhere with me. I changed my attitude, reaction, expectation, and words I chose to use. - Ashley

You could be keeping score and not even realize it. But by learning how to communicate with your spouse, you will be in a better position to not keep score.

I used to keep score during the first few months of our marriage. I did it primarily because I was comparing everything I did with what Ashley did.

I thought we should split everything up equally, 50-50, but that isn't always the case.

There will be times when I have to do most of the chores at home because Ashley is sick or busy multitasking for our own good. It's in these times that I realized keeping score was devastating to our marriage and myself. — Marcus

Some Simple Mistakes You Should Watch Out For When Communicating With Your Spouse

- ❖ Miscommunication.
- ❖ Assuming.
- ❖ Criticism.
- ❖ Blaming and accusing your spouse.
- ❖ Quick temperament- anger.
- ❖ Yelling, or raising your voice.
- ❖ Sarcasm.
- ❖ Name-calling.
- ❖ Not communicating to your spouse how you feel, thus allowing things to fester and build resentment.
- ❖ Misunderstanding each other.
- ❖ Different marriage expectations.
- ❖ Not asking for clarification.
- ❖ Previous unresolved conflicts.
- ❖ Difference in opinions.
- ❖ Disagreement on how to spend money.

When Are The Best Times To Not Try To Communicate With Your Spouse?

❖ Right after your spouse gets back from work, a busy event, or from a distressing experience.

❖ When they are not in a good mood to talk. We all have good and bad days. During those bad days it may not be the best time to talk about the important issues. But do not use this as an excuse to not talk about the issues in your marriage. The earlier you solve them, the better your marriage will be. Set a time aside to talk.

❖ When you are stressed. Stress can heavily impact how you communicate. Therefore, when you are stressed, talk only about things that will help you relieve stress. There is no benefit to adding more stress to what you are already experiencing.

❖ When you are in a rush. It's not a good time at all. Your spouse will not be able to listen to you properly when you are talking and walking out the door so you don't get to work late.

Ask your spouse and yourself:

1. Do you feel that you have to be right?

2. Do you think everything can have more than one way to get done, or have more than one solution to a problem?

3. Do you argue about the same topic often? If so, what's the root of that disagreement?

4. Do you keep score?

5. What is one thing you can do to create a new way of communicating through disagreements today?

CHAPTER 6

It's Not Possible Without Trust

Trust is a vital part of communication. Without trust, a healthy marriage relationship cannot exist. Without trust, communication with each other will not be as effective. Can you believe what your spouse says if you do not trust them?

Trust issues in marriage can be caused through physical affairs, lying, emotional affairs, contact with an ex, use of pornography, etc. The lack of trust usually breeds insecurity. Therefore, building complete trust in your marriage should be a priority as it leads to a deeper level of healthy communication. Being able to trust your husband or wife completely provides you with the comfort and freedom to express yourself. Trust gives you the ability to feel secure enough to share every part of yourself with your spouse without fear of rejection or being ashamed. In the same way your spouse needs to be able to trust that the deep intimate things you talk about and share with each other, stay between the two of you.

"Intimacy comes from "knowing" the other person at a deep level. If there are barriers to honesty, knowing is ruled out and the false takes over." (Boundaries in Marriage.)

In order for you both to feel safe enough to bare your souls to each other, to be naked emotionally with your spouse, and communicate better, you must cultivate mutual trust. Truly knowing someone, having them know you, being truly loved and accepted for who you are, is one of the best things marriage can offer. Being that deeply connected with another human being, gives us purpose in life. As humans we will do anything for that connection, which is why some turn to addictive behaviors.

"Human beings have a deep need to bond and form connections. It's how we get our satisfaction. If we can't connect with each other, we will connect with anything we can find."(Johann Hari)

Building trust in marriage does not happen overnight. It simply takes time and purpose. It will require some extra effort if either you or your spouse have had trust issues from past relationships.

Start by making sure you are being completely honest with your spouse. Do you have anything you haven't told your spouse about your past, present, or even future plans? In order to make complete trust a reality in your marriage, make sure you are being trustworthy. Tell your spouse when you overspend on an item from the budget. If you feel like you have started entertaining thoughts about another person than your spouse, or feel you may have done something you wouldn't want your spouse doing if roles were reversed, simply have a conversation to discuss it.

When you are hurt by something, when you didn't do something you said you would, and the list goes on. Be an open book with your spouse. Share your secrets, especially the pains and struggles you go through every day. Don't be afraid to ask them questions. It won't be easy all the time, but the more you establish trust, the more you will become completely open and connected with your spouse. Never threaten your spouse! When you do this, they will feel hurt and not safe around you. This will result in them not being as open with you. Try your best to never say things to purposely hurt your spouse for the sake of injury.

You can't be afraid to rock the boat and hide things or stuff down your feelings. It means you're not only lying to your spouse, but yourself. Stuffing things down inside you and not being able to properly express your emotions in a healthy way can be hazardous to your health, as well as your relationship. By not getting it out in the open, you are letting it build up, which will become resentment towards your spouse. If you let all these little things pile up, you will eventually explode over something trivial. When you bottle up your emotions, they turn into anger and resentment. If you can't be honest and emotionally vulnerable with your spouse, or they you, there is something deeper going on that is hindering that honest communication.

Can one little white lie really do much harm to a marriage? What about lying by omission? No harm, no foul right? Wrong. The answer is simple. Lies, or not telling your spouse the truth because what they don't know won't hurt them, erodes the basic foundation of your marriage, which is trust. It makes you feel guilty and makes it impossible to be truly intimate on a deeper level.

"Deception damages a relationship. The act of lying is much more damaging than the things that are being lied about, because lying undermines the knowing of one another and the connection itself...Deception is the one thing that cannot be worked through because it denies the problem." -Dr. Henry Cloud.

You may be thinking, that's an overload of information to share, what if you forget something? These are just examples to help you better understand the small areas. You can start by making sure that you are being trustworthy to your spouse. If your spouse tells you something, they have to know that it is going to stay between the two of you. If you have an argument, don't go run to your best friend or family member. Nine times out of ten, it is because of a miscommunication. When you run to a family member, parents, or friend, they will see your spouse in another light, and that you can't take back so easily. They don't love your spouse like you do.

**Again, the exception to this is if your spouse does or says harmful or abusive things.

Once you learn how to communicate with your spouse, and understand the importance of trust in marriage, it will become easier to approach your spouse because you will be talking to your best friend, who you have established an intimate relationship with. You need to be honest with your spouse, and your spouse needs to be honest with you.

Take the first steps to establish trust by communicating to your spouse that you need to be honest with each other even if it hurts, and it will hurt sometimes. We had a few incidences in our first year of marriage where complete honesty was not present and we hurt each other in the process, unintentionally. We worked through this by communicating, explaining that this wasn't okay. We wouldn't accept it in our marriage, and forgave each other.

Did we mess up again? Absolutely. When you are this close to someone, everything you do directly affects your spouse, and everything they do affects you. We are not perfect and never will be. All we can do is strive to be better every day, learn from our mistakes and the mistakes of others who share their wisdom, and move on.

Your trust for each other must be *nurtured* and *protected* continually. It's very hard to rebuild trust in marriage, therefore *respect* the trust your spouse has for you, and never take it for granted.

"In marriage, we have the opportunity to have the most intimate relationship with another human being; our spouse." Dr. Henry Cloud.

You may be wondering why we are talking about trust in a book about communication. The truth is, you will not be able to communicate effectively without trust. To enjoy the gift that marriage makes possible, of such a rich and deep communication, where neither you nor your spouse is afraid to be completely naked emotionally and effusive with each other, requires trust.

The love making will benefit when you completely trust your spouse too!

Tips For Cultivating Trust In Your Marriage

❖ Ask your spouse what you can do to earn their trust.

❖ Promise yourself and each other that you will be truthful and honest even if it hurts.

❖ Share your secrets, especially the pains and struggles you go through every day. Be emotionally vulnerable.

❖ Stop the lying, by omission or otherwise.

❖ Be aware of the damages caused, accept your wrong doings and be responsible.

❖ Keep your promises.

❖ Listen and pay attention to your spouse.

❖ *Give your spouse an opportunity to earn your trust.*

❖ Trust in marriage is mutual; it takes two to make it happen.

❖ Be yourself and be real.

❖ Be open to counseling or seeing a marriage coach if need be.

❖ It will take time and patience--a lot of patience.

❖ Show your spouse you love and appreciate them.

❖ Set boundaries in your marriage to prevent a repeat of the same issues that caused trust to be broken.

Ask yourself and your spouse:

1. Are you completely honest with your spouse?

2. Is there a question you have been wanting to ask your spouse for some time?

3. Do you keep your feelings hidden about anything?

4. Do you feel you can be completely honest with each other?

5. Do you feel safe with your spouse?

6. Do you feel accepted by your spouse in every way? If not, how can you work towards that?

7. What is one thing you can do to earn your spouse's trust?

CHAPTER 7

7 Simple Steps for Getting Started

How do you begin communicating with your spouse? This can be a daunting task especially when your spouse does not want to talk with you. But look no further; the steps below can help you communicate with your spouse even if you do not know where to start. It will also help you improve communication in your marriage when things are not going well. And it starts with you putting into action the seven simple steps we share below. We have used these simple steps several times to improve communication in our marriage, and we have had great successes. Honestly, we believe these communication strategies will help you get started on communicating better with your spouse today.

Even if your spouse is not willing to practice them with you, you can practice them every day, and it will make your marriage better.

1. May I have your attention, please? This is where you practice active listening. Make sure both you and your spouse are listening and paying attention when you have a conversation with each other. If your spouse is not listening, or paying attention, all your "words" will not be heard. When your spouse is saying something to you, stop and listen to them. They will appreciate you listening. Actually listen, not just hear. All you have to do is listen attentively to everything your spouse says to you. Don't interrupt while they talk, and put away distractions. It's very easy to be distracted these days due to how "busy" we all are. Distractions make it very difficult to communicate, especially when it comes to listening, paying full attention, and being engaged in the conversation. The environment you are in impacts how you communicate. A great place to start is by asking your spouse when a good time would be to have their undivided attention. Make sure it is not when your spouse is too tired, stressed, or emotionally charged.

2. No yelling. Do not yell at your spouse when you are trying to convey a message or talking to each other. It simply does not set the tone for effective communication. Do you want your spouse to yell at you? Ironically, we yell to be heard, but it only encourages your spouse to yell back or completely shut down. Talk to them how you want to be talked to, in a calm and respectful tone. If you feel you are getting too emotional or angry, take a break and revisit when you are both calm. Be respectful and loving with your tone.

3. A mile in your spouse's shoes. Whenever you are having a discussion, argument, or just talking, try to see the issue from your spouse's point of view. Try to understand where your spouse is coming from, and practice empathetic listening. This will enable you to understand what your spouse is trying to communicate to you. How would your spouse best understand what you are trying to communicate to them? Remember they think differently than you.

4. Confirm understanding. Clarify! Ask your spouse if they understand what you are trying to communicate with them. Let them describe it to you if they understand you clearly. What words are they using? What does the word mean? This works to help you see where they are with understanding what you're trying to convey. *Don't say everything is fine when you know something is wrong.* Mean what you say to your spouse. If you are in a noisy environment, it makes it difficult to hear, let alone listen and understand what the other person is saying. Make sure the environment you are in is good enough to hear each other clearly, to be able to understand, and communicate well. When you do not hear something, do not be scared to ask. It's better to ask now, rather than later.

5. Change your style and hit the home run. When your spouse does not understand something you said, try explaining it to them using different ways. Depending on what you are trying to communicate, try different verbal explanations, analogies, or even pictures. You could also use the drawing of diagrams, writing on paper, etc. If you do not understand anything, or did not hear something your spouse said, do not be shy. Ask them to repeat what they said and explain it in a way you will understand.

6. Take a break. If you are not making progress communicating a thought, idea, a problem, or you begin to feel frustrated, take a break. Revisit later after you have each had time to think about the issue. This is so important and extremely helpful. Sometimes we just need time to re-evaluate.

7. Rinse and repeat. Apply the above strategies every time you communicate with your spouse. Remember, the key is to be open-minded, listen attentively, and have patience!

These seven strategies are proven from our life and marriage experience. And we encourage you to apply them to communicate better with your spouse. We have used and continue to use these simple steps to communicate effectively with each other. They work!

In order to improve communication in any marriage, the desire and willingness of the couple is required. Therefore, you need to understand it will take intentional effort from you and your spouse to communicate effectively in your marriage.

In addition, by knowing how to communicate better with your spouse, you can prevent most of the communication issues, and petty (even some big) arguments in your marriage.

Check out the 7-day action plan we created below to help you learn how to communicate with your spouse. We also created a list of excellent resources on the last page to help you improve your marriage.

Your 7-Day Action Plan

For the next seven days, implement all the 7 simple steps every single day. Yes, every time you speak or communicate with your spouse. To make it even better, implement them whenever you communicate with someone, whether you are at work, the supermarket, or grocery store. To make it easier, start with one or two things at a time, like working on your tone while speaking to your spouse and listening emphatically to them.

These steps have worked very well for us and will work for you, too. The only thing needed is your desire to implement them. If your spouse is not willing to communicate with you, we highly suggest you seek the help of a professional.

Visit www.ourpeacefulfamily.com/7dayworksheet to get your copy of the 7-Day Worksheet we created to make it easier for you to practice the steps.

Final Thoughts

If you are having communication problems with your spouse, what is preventing you from learning the communication skills needed to communicate with them?

We hope you can apply the strategies and advice from this comprehensive book to cultivate effective communication in your marriage. The whole reason we wrote this book is to help give you the tools to communicate better with your spouse.

This is where you decide to take a deep breath and put your work boots on. This is going to be harder for some couples and easier for others. The important thing is that you start. Make an effort to work on adding one thing at a time, and eventually a lot of this will become second nature because it's the beginning of you changing the culture of your marriage relationship.

Good luck, and have fun growing in this together!

Short Q & A

How to express your feelings and needs without attacking your spouse:

"I am not saying you are doing this to make me feel this way, but when you do x I feel…"

Try using non-accusatory words and an understanding calm tone when trying to communicate with your spouse. Ask for solutions. Make your spouse feel important. What can they do to make this better? More importantly, what can you do to make this better?

What to do when you are upset, overwhelmed, or emotions are running hot:

Learn to recognize when you start to feel the anger or frustration rising. Learn to pause and take a moment to think about what you want to say and do before you respond. Learn to know when you need to take a break, whether that means five minutes or an hour. Learn to not blame your spouse.

What do you do when your spouse does not want to talk or communicate with you? When they are silent?

Give them space. Tell them you would like to talk to them about something when they are ready. Tell them to let you know when they are prepared. Remember to be respectful and loving.

How to receive criticisms without getting defensive:

This can be very hard in the beginning. You can ask your spouse to give you two things right for every one thing they need to critique. Or maybe space out the helpful critiques.

How to identify communication problems and fix it:

Find the root cause. What is the common theme of the arguments? Miscommunication? Do you not feel you are being loved or respected in some way? What is your Love Language? What is your spouse's Love Language?

How should we work together as a team when solving different problems and communicating with each other?

Keep in the back of your mind two things: First, your spouse has the best intentions for you, and they wouldn't purposely try to do you harm. Second, you need to treat each other as you want to be treated with the same understanding, love, and respect.

Thank you

Congratulations on reading this far! We are very thankful and excited to help you learn how to communicate with your spouse and build a strong foundation for your marriage.

If you enjoyed reading this book, please leave us a review and rating on Amazon.

We would both love to know how this book impacts you and your marriage and what we can do to make this book better.

You can send us an email about any questions you have about communication in marriage to:

firstyearmarriage@gmail.com.

We cannot promise that we will immediately reply every email due to the volume of emails we receive, but we will do our best to cover your question in future blog posts or podcast episodes.

If you would like to receive email updates about future books, bonuses, plus get your FREE 7-Day Worksheet, visit the website: **www.ourpeacefulfamily.com/7dayworksheet**

Thank you again for choosing and reading our book!

Marcus and Ashley Kusi

Enjoy your marriage, enjoy your life!

References

Van Marwijk., Frank. "Everyone Uses Body Language." Www.lichaamstaal.com. Web. http://www.lichaamstaal.com/english

Eggerichs, Emerson. Love & Respect: The Love She Most Desires, the Respect He Desperately Needs. Nashville, TN: Integrity ;, 2004. Print.

Cloud, Henry, and John Sims Townsend. Boundaries in Marriage. Grand Rapids, MI: ZondervanPublishingHouse, 1999. Print.

Hari, Johann. "The Likely Cause of Addiction Has Been Discovered, and It Is Not What You Think." The Huffington Post. TheHuffingtonPost.com. Web. 22 Feb. 2015. http://www.huffingtonpost.com/johann-hari/the-real-cause-of-addicti_b_6506936.html

Excellent Resources

If you have not yet read the books below, we highly recommend you get a copy from your local library or buy one online.

1. The Five Love Languages by Dr. Gary Smalley.
2. Love and Respect by Dr. Emerson Eggerichs.
3. Boundaries In Marriage by Dr. Henry Cloud.

You should also check out the list of excellent marriage resources we recommend for couples by visiting our website: **www.ourpeacefulfamily.com/resources**